Safety

Crabtree Publishing Company

www.crabtreebooks.com

Crabtree Publishing Company

www.crabtreebooks.com   1-800-387-7650

Copyright © **2009 CRABTREE PUBLISHING COMPANY.**

Published in Canada
Crabtree Publishing
616 Welland Ave.
St. Catharines, ON
L2M 5V6

Published in the United States
Crabtree Publishing
PMB16A
350 Fifth Ave., Suite 3308
New York, NY 10118

Senior editor
Jennifer Schofield

Proofreader
Crystal Sikkens

Designer
Sophie Pelham

Project coordinator
Robert Walker

Digital color
Carl Gordon

Production coordinator
Margaret Amy Salter

Editor
Molly Aloian

Prepress technician
Katherine Kantor

Copy editor
Adrianna Morganelli

First published in 2008 by Wayland
338 Euston Road
London NW1 3BH

Wayland Australia
Level 17/207 Kent Street
Sydney NSW 2000

Copyright © Wayland 2008

Wayland is a division of
Hachette Children's Books,
a Hachette Livre UK company.

Library and Archives Canada Cataloguing in Publication

Gogerly, Liz
    Safety / Liz Gogerly ; illustrator, Mike Gordon.

(Looking after me)
Includes index.
ISBN 978-0-7787-4113-8 (bound).--ISBN 978-0-7787-4120-6 (pbk.)
.

    1. Safety education--Juvenile fiction. I. Gordon, Mike II. Title.
III. Series: Gogerly, Liz. Looking after me.

PZ7.G562Sa 2008   j823'.92   C2008-903645-X

Library of Congress Cataloging-in-Publication Data

Gogerly, Liz.
    Safety / written by Liz Gogerly ; illustrated by Mike Gordon.
        p. cm. -- (Looking after me)
    Includes index.
    ISBN-13: 978-0-7787-4113-8 (reinforced library binding : alk. paper)
    ISBN-10: 0-7787-4113-3 (reinforced library binding : alk. paper)
    ISBN-13: 978-0-7787-4120-6 (pbk. : alk. paper)
    ISBN-10: 0-7787-4120-6 (pbk. : alk. paper)
    1. Safety education--Juvenile literature. 2. Children's accidents--
Prevention--Juvenile literature. I. Gordon, Mike, ill. II. Title. III. Series.

    HQ770.7.G63 2009
    613.6083--dc22
                                                    2008025347

Looking After Me

Safety

Written by Liz Gogerly
Illustrated by Mike Gordon

Going to the park
was my idea of fun.

Dad said it was his idea of a nightmare.

5

The troubles usually began on the way to the park. I wanted to get there VERY quickly.

I never bothered to STOP,
LOOK, and LISTEN when
I crossed the street.

As soon as we got
to the park, I was off.
Sometimes, I pretended to be
a daredevil pilot...

Until I landed in dog poop.

Another time I
pretended I was
a champion
ice skater.

10

I whizzed around and around, but my poor dog fell in the ice. I didn't skate again!

I pretended to be a world-famous mountain climber, too. The other kid was OK but I got a bump on my head.

I didn't climb up the slide the wrong way again.

Dad always said he didn't know what was going to happen next when we were at the park.

Don't pick up sharp things, Molly!

He said there was always an accident just waiting to happen.

15

He told me it was dangerous
to go up to strangers' dogs,
but I never listened to him.

Then, a dog got angry
with me.

I didn't touch strange
dogs again.

One day, I really wished I'd listened to my Dad. He always told me to stay where he could see me, and I could see him.

He also told me to be careful of strangers.

At first, the man outside
the store seemed friendly.

But then I got a funny feeling...
I thought he was lying.

HELP ME!

I shouted loudly, but nobody came.

So, I pretended I was an Olympic runner. I ran and ran and ran.

I was lucky.

The man wasn't behind me.
But I was lost.

Dad told me that if I was ever lost, I should find a grownup with other kids, or a police officer, but I couldn't see anyone I trusted.

Dad also said I could ask for help in a store, a library, or another place I already knew.

Luckily, I remembered my address and telephone number.

And very soon, Mom and Dad came to get me.

Now I listen to my parents and I try to keep safe.

I'm going to the moon.

I also tell my Mom and Dad where I'm going.

But I still have a lot of adventures.

NOTES FOR PARENTS AND TEACHERS

SUGGESTIONS FOR READING
LOOKING AFTER ME: SAFETY
WITH CHILDREN

Safety is the story of an energetic and adventurous young girl named Molly. At the start of the book, we read about Molly in a variety of situations that could be dangerous. She is in such a rush to get to the park that she forgets the basic rules of road safety. This would be a good opportunity to ask the children about what they know about road safety. Afterward, you could talk to them about how they should behave when there is traffic. Another point worth raising is remembering to slow down and think about what you are doing, whatever the situation may be.

Molly's trip to the park is filled with safety issues for children. Trees, frozen ponds, playground rides, and dogs all threaten children's safety. Let the children talk about these everyday hazards. Perhaps there are other safety issues that have not been covered in this story that they have experienced. In the section where Molly discovers "treasure," which is actually broken glass, you could broaden the discussion to include other sharp objects, such as discarded needles or dangerous objects in the house.

One of the most important things we can teach children is what to do if they encounter a stranger. Molly has a gut reaction about the man in the store. Children often know when something or someone feels strange and it's important that they act on those feelings. Molly listens to her own feelings and makes her escape. Talk about this situation with the children and discuss what they would and should do in a similar situation.

In this story, Molly also has to cope with being lost. Fortunately, she did listen to her father's advice and followed his instructions. This is an opportunity to find out how the children would react in a similar situation. It is also a good time to urge the children to learn their full names, addresses, and telephone numbers in case of an emergency.

LOOKING AFTER ME AND CURRICULUM EXPECTATIONS

The Looking After Me series is designed to teach young readers the importance of personal hygiene, proper nutrition, exercise, and personal safety. This series supports key K-4 health education standards in Canada and the United States, including those outlined by the American Association for Health Education. According to these standards, students will

- Describe relationships between personal health behaviors and individual well being
- Explain how childhood injuries and illnesses can be prevented or treated
- Identify responsible health behaviors
- Identify personal health needs
- Demonstrate strategies to improve or maintain personal health
- Demonstrate ways to avoid and reduce threatening situations

BOOKS TO READ

I Can be Safe: A First Look at Safety
Pat Thomas (Wayland, 2004)

Once Upon a Dragon: Stranger Safety for Kids (and Dragons)
Jean E. Pendziwol (Kids Can Press, 2006)

Look Out on the Road
Claire Llewellyn (Wayland, 2006)

ACTIVITY

Ask the children to identify methods of making the area around their school or home safe. For example, cycle routes, sidewalks, fences, no parking zones, road signs, pedestrian crossings. Do they think each of these methods is important? Do they work? How could they make the areas safer?

INDEX

32

Printed in China